CONTENTS

PLACES TO
CONQUER

INTRODUCTION

This book describes some of the toughest warriors of all time, from conquering medieval kings to brilliant Roman generals. Some of them were brave, some were ruthless, and others were wickedly clever. But they all were as hard as nails.

FIND OUT ABOUT . . .

- The conqueror whose skull ended up as a cup

- A pair of rebel sisters who ruled Vietnam

- The British prime minister who fought in a duel

- A female samurai warrior

If you've ever wanted to ride a war elephant or fire a trebuchet, read on. Follow the warriors through a freezing Russian winter, across the Rubicon river, and into the mountains of Mexico.

As well as discovering stories of courage and cunning, you might be in for a few surprises. Did you know, for example, that the Ming dynasty was started by a starving peasant? Or that Cyrus the Great commanded soldiers mounted on dromedary camels?

You're about to meet some of the toughest warriors in history . . .

Plus play the game on page 36 and see if you've got what it takes to conquer an enormous empire!

CYRUS THE GREAT

HARD AS NAILS RATING: 8.3

Cyrus the Great was a warrior king with a talent for conquering. He founded the mighty Persian Empire, the largest of its time.

DEFEATING THE MEDIANS

When Cyrus became King of Persia in 559 BCE, Persia was part of the Median Empire. Cyrus didn't like being ruled by the Median leader, Astyages, or anyone else for that matter, so he rebelled. He defeated Astyages and captured the capital city of Ecbatana. Now Cyrus was the ruler of the Median Empire, which he liked much better.

BATTERING THE LYDIANS

Croesus, king of Lydia, worried that Cyrus was becoming too powerful and made the mistake of marching his army against him. Cyrus defeated Croesus at the Battle of Sardis,

CONQUERING LIST

using soldiers mounted on dromedary camels, which frightened the Lydian horses. He ordered King Croesus to be burned to death—though there are stories that he might have changed his mind—and added Lydia to his realm.

KING OF THE WORLD

Next on Cyrus's conquering list was the Elam civilization, followed by Babylonia. He dealt with them both swiftly and easily, but with plenty of bloodshed. Afterward, he modestly declared himself king of Babylon, king of Sumer and Akkad, and king of the Four Corners of the World. It wasn't actually that much of an exaggeration.

MESSING WITH THE MASSAGETAE

Cyrus realized that the Massagetae, just to the north of his great empire, remained unconquered. He added them to his list. Cyrus tried an unusual tactic: he asked their leader, Tomyris, to marry him. Wisely, she refused. So Cyrus led his warriors against the Massagetae army. But Cyrus was in for a big shock. The Persians were defeated and Cyrus was killed. The story goes that Queen Tomyris used his skull as a drinking cup (see page 42).

MIGHTY EMPIRE

Cyrus conquered a territory that stretched all the way from the Mediterranean to what's now Pakistan, and founded an empire that would last more than 200 years. His son, Cambyses II, conquered Egypt and made the Persian Empire even bigger.

HARDOMETER

CUNNING: 9
COURAGE: 9
SURVIVAL SKILLS: 6
RUTHLESSNESS: 9

BABUR

Babur was a warrior who fought for and conquered an empire—the Moghul Empire in India.

HARD AS NAILS RATING: 8.5

KICKED OUT

Babur's distant relatives included Genghis Khan and Timur (see pages 12 and 52). With family members like that, it was no surprise that he enjoyed conquering. In 1495, when Babur was 12, he became ruler of Farghana, an area that's now in Uzbekistan. His uncles did their best to kick him off the throne, and he was forced to live in exile. But Babur didn't let them stop him from conquering.

SEIZING SAMARKAND

Two years later, after a long siege, Babur captured the city that his father had tried to capture for years: Samarkand. Feeling confident, he marched on Farghana to take his throne—but his army was defeated. To make matters worse, the troops he'd left behind in newly captured Samarkand were attacked and defeated while he was away. Babur was left with nothing.

CAPTURING KABUL

In 1504, now a 21-year-old with a strong army, Babur captured the city of Kabul (in what's now Afghanistan) and gained a new and wealthy kingdom. This was more like it. Babur fought his old enemies, the Uzbeks. He had to crush a rebellion in Kabul, and was over time driven out of the city by revolting generals. But over time he recaptured the city.

TIMUR

GENGHIS KHAN

INVADING INDIA

Babur began making raids into India in 1519, keeping a greedy eye on its land and wealth. He made more raids over the next few years, but didn't stay in India until his victory at the first Battle of Panipat, against the sultan of Delhi, in 1526. He captured Delhi and marched to Agra. Babur was now surrounded by hostile enemies, but he managed to defeat them and conquer an Indian empire.

MOGHUL EMPIRE

Babur's new empire covered most of northern India, with its capital at Agra. His son and grandson made the Moghul Empire even larger, and the Moghuls ruled for more than 300 years after Babur died.

HARDOMETER

CUNNING: 9
COURAGE: 8
SURVIVAL SKILLS: 9
RUTHLESSNESS: 8

GENGHIS KHAN

Genghis Khan led a rampaging horseback army in Mongolia and beyond, and built an empire that became the second-largest in the history of the world.

A BAD BEGINNING

Genghis Khan was born in the Gobi desert in Mongolia around 1162. He was the son of a chief, but when he was nine his father was murdered. Genghis and the rest of his family were exiled. Things got even worse when a group of their enemies captured Genghis and held him prisoner, but he made a daring escape and earned a reputation for bravery in the process.

MONGOLS UNITED

Genghis married the daughter of another chief, and his powerful new family and hard as nails reputation earned him followers. He soon discovered he liked being in charge, and decided to unite the peoples of Mongolia, who were constantly fighting one another, and put himself in charge of all of them.

HARDOMETER

CUNNING: 8
COURAGE: 8
SURVIVAL SKILLS: 9
RUTHLESSNESS: 9

UNIVERSAL LEADER

Genghis managed to persuade or bully the different Mongol groups into uniting. Sometimes he was heavy-handed—when one group of Mongols wouldn't do as he wanted, he killed all its adults. By 1206, all of Mongolia was united, and he was given the name Genghis Khan, which

means universal leader—
until then he'd been
called Temujin.

CONQUERING

Genghis formed a tough,
disciplined, horseback-
mounted army from the
united Mongols. They
were deadly accurate
archers and terrifying
warriors. Genghis led
them on a conquering
spree, starting with
northwestern China,
and continuing into
other parts of central
Asia, Russia,
and India.

EXPANDING EMPIRE

Genghis and his
Mongolian army were
extremely successful.
His empire stretched
all the way from
modern-day Poland
and Turkey in the west
to southeast Asia and the coast of China in the east. After
he died in 1227, Genghis's grandson, Kublai Khan, and
later generations made the empire even bigger. It was the
second-biggest empire ever, after the British Empire in the
twentieth century.

THE TRUNG SISTERS

The Trung sisters were
Vietnamese heroines
who rebelled against their
Chinese rulers, and ended up
running the country.

HARD AS
NAILS
RATING: 7.8

CHINESE RULERS

Vietnam was ruled by the Chinese Han dynasty when the
Trung sisters, Trung Trac and Trung Nhi, were born around
10 CE. Their father was a powerful lord, and they grew up in
a time when Vietnamese women were allowed to become
leaders, warriors, businesswomen, and judges. The sisters
studied martial arts and grew up tough.

STARTING A REBELLION

Foreign rule was bad enough, but
when the Chinese killed Trung
Trac's husband, the Trung sisters
decided to do something
about it. They persuaded
the Vietnamese lords to
start a rebellion against
the Chinese rulers. The
story goes that the sisters
performed acts of bravery
to show how tough they
were. One of these daring
deeds included killing a
fierce, man-eating tiger, and
writing a proclamation on
its skin telling everyone
to rise up against their
foreign rulers.

REBEL ARMY

The Trung sisters must have been very persuasive, because they ended up with an army of 80,000 soldiers. They were trained to be terrifying warriors. The Trungs chose 36 women to be army generals. The Vietnamese army marched against the Chinese army, with the Trung sisters bravely leading the way. They captured 65 cities held by the Chinese, and drove their enemies out of Vietnam in 40 CE.

TRUNGS IN CHARGE

The people of Vietnam celebrated the victory, and proclaimed the Trung sisters as joint queens. They ruled Vietnam for the next three years. Not surprisingly, the Chinese weren't happy that they'd been thrown out of Vietnam, so they attacked the country to try and win it back. No matter how bravely and fiercely the Trungs and the Vietnamese fought, the Chinese army was bigger and better equipped. In 43 CE, the Chinese finally won.

EVADING CAPTURE

Instead of being captured by the Chinese, the Trung sisters chose to kill themselves. One legend says that they drowned themselves. The sisters became national heroes, and are still remembered in poems, songs, and art.

HARDOMETER

CUNNING: 8
COURAGE: 9
SURVIVAL SKILLS: 6
RUTHLESSNESS: 8

HARD AS NAILS WOMEN

Most really famous warriors are men, but there are also plenty of hard as nails women. Boudica, Joan of Arc, Tomyris, Tomoe Gozen, and the Trung sisters are all featured in this book. Here are a few more tough female fighters from throughout history.

ARTEMISIA

Artemisia was queen of Halicarnassus. Today, it's in Turkey, but in the 400s BCE it was part of the Persian Empire. Persian emperor Xerxes I invaded Greece, and fought the Greeks in a famous sea battle at Salamis. Artemisia commanded her own fleet of five ships for the Persians, and put all the male Persian commanders to shame with her skill and bravery.

CLEOPATRA

Cleopatra ruled Egypt with her younger brother, but she was kicked out because she wanted to rule on her own. With the help of a powerful Roman boyfriend, Julius Caesar, she got rid of her brother. After Caesar died, Cleopatra made a brave attempt at grabbing the entire Roman Empire, by declaring that her son with Caesar was the true heir. Her plan, hatched with another Roman boyfriend, didn't work out. She killed herself by letting a venomous snake bite her.

ZENOBIA

Zenobia was queen of Palmyra in Syria. In 269 CE, she conquered Egypt, and went on to conquer a large part of Anatolia (in what's now Turkey) and chunks of land in the Middle East. She was known as a brilliant horse rider and a brave warrior. The Romans finally defeated Zenobia in battle and captured her, despite her daring escape attempt by camel.

GRACE O'MALLEY

Grace was an Irish leader who controlled her coastline by becoming a pirate in the 1500s. She was ruthless and brave, and grew wealthy from her work on the seas. She also defeated her English enemies, pouring hot lead on their heads when they attacked her castle.

FLORA SANDES

Flora was one of only two British women to fight in the First World War. She joined an ambulance service and was sent to Serbia, where she enlisted in the Serbian army (there were a few other Serbian women soldiers, too). Flora was wounded in 1916 and received a medal for bravery.

KING PIYE

**Piye was a warrior king
who invaded and conquered
Egypt, and founded a
new Egyptian dynasty.**

KUSHY JOB

Piye ruled a kingdom to the south of Egypt, called Kush,
in the 700s BCE. In ancient times, Kush was part of Nubia
(today it would be in Sudan). Hundreds of years before
Piye was the king of Kush, all of Egypt had been ruled by
powerful pharaohs. In King Piye's time, Egypt was split into
territories, each ruled by different leaders.

CONQUERING UPPER EGYPT

King Piye had a perfectly good kingdom of his own, but the
fertile lands of Egypt were not far away, and he couldn't
resist paying the country a visit. And he took his army with
him. It wasn't long before he'd conquered Upper Egypt—
the southern part of the country. Piye's sister was accepted
as a priestess of the god Amun-Re, who was worshiped by
the Kushites as well as the Egyptians. The role was both
political and religious, and meant that Piye now controlled
even more land.

HARDOMETER

CUNNING: 9
COURAGE: 9
SURVIVAL SKILLS: 9
RUTHLESSNESS: 9

DELTA ALLIANCE

At the Nile Delta in Lower Egypt,
where the Nile River meets the
Mediterranean Sea, there were
several different leaders. One
of them in particular, Tefnakht,
didn't like Piye's conquering
ways—he was becoming far too
powerful for Tefnakht's liking.

So he got together with a group of the other Nile Delta leaders and formed an army against the Kushite king.

CONQUERING LOWER EGYPT

Piye led his warriors into battle. He marched north and defeated the allied leaders' army. Just to show everyone he really was in charge, he captured cities in the north of Egypt, including Memphis, the ancient Egyptian capital. Now he had conquered Lower Egypt as well as Upper Egypt.

PIYE RULES

The Nile delta leaders admitted they were beaten, and accepted that Piye was now in control of their lands—except for Tefnakht, who ran away. Piye was in charge of Egypt until he died in 716 BCE. He never became pharaoh of Egypt, but his son and heir to his throne did, starting a new Kushite dynasty.

GERONIMO

Geronimo was a fearless Apache warrior who gained a terrifying reputation from his enemies.

HARD AS NAILS RATING: 8.3

AT WAR WITH THE SETTLERS

Geronimo was part of a group of Apaches who lived in what's now the state of Arizona in the United States. By the time he was born in 1829, Europeans had already been settled in the United States for hundreds of years, and the indigenous peoples were being moved out of their homelands. Some of them, including Geronimo's group of Apaches, made raids on the settlers to try and drive them out, and the settlers fought back.

RAIDERS

Geronimo was away trading when a group of Mexican soldiers raided his camp. When he returned with the other men, they found that many of the women and children had been murdered, including Geronimo's mother, wife, and three children. After that, Geronimo's attacks on the Mexicans became more frequent and more violent, and he soon earned a reputation as a fearless warrior. One story says he braved a hail of bullets to attack Mexican soldiers with a knife. He became leader of his group of Apache warriors.

HARDOMETER

CUNNING: 7
COURAGE: 9
SURVIVAL SKILLS: 8
RUTHLESSNESS: 9

APACHE RESERVATION

In 1874, thousands of Apaches were moved by the United States government off their land and onto a reservation in Arizona. The land was barren and the people were miserable. Hundreds of them followed Geronimo out of the reservation and became outlaws, continuing their war against the settlers. But eventually, in 1884, Geronimo surrendered.

ESCAPE

In 1885, Geronimo ran away from the reservation again, but he was tracked down by the United States army in Mexico, and he surrendered. As they approached the border to the United States, Geronimo was worried that his Apache band of warriors would be killed once they were in United States territory—and so he made another bid to escape!

CAPTURED AGAIN

More than 5,000 men set off in pursuit of Geronimo and his small group of warriors. After five months, the Apaches were tracked down to their camp in Mexico. Geronimo was persuaded to surrender again, and he was promised that he could soon return to Arizona. It wasn't true. First Geronimo was imprisoned, then he was sent to a new reservation in Oklahoma. But Geronimo's fighting days were over. He lived peacefully, and wrote a book about his life.

JULIUS CAESAR

Julius Caesar is one of the most famous warriors of all time. His military conquests helped make him the most powerful person in the ancient Roman world.

HARD AS NAILS RATING: 8.3

EXILE AND HOMECOMING

Caesar was born into a wealthy Roman family in 100 BCE, but he was forced to live in exile. The brutal Roman dictator, Sulla, was an old family enemy and he was busy killing anyone he didn't like in Rome. When Julius Caesar returned to Rome after Sulla's death, Caesar's charm and reputation won him several top jobs in politics. As governor of Spain, Caesar led his troops in an invasion of what's now Portugal, which was very successful and made him even more popular. The Romans were big fans of conquering heroes.

GALLIC WARS

Even though Julius Caesar now held the most important job in Rome, he wasn't happy. He seized power with two friends, Pompey and Crassus. Then he went off to Gaul (modern-day France and Belgium) in search of some more territory. It took him eight years, but he succeeded in conquering all of it and adding a huge chunk to the empire, along with plenty of treasure and slaves. He was so impressed with his own conquests that he wrote a book about his time in Gaul, *The Gallic Wars*.

CIVIL WAR

The three-man leadership of Rome didn't work out. Crassus was killed, and Caesar fought with Pompey. They argued over who should be in charge of Rome. The politicians backed Pompey, but Caesar had the advantage of an army, brilliant battle tactics, and a single-minded lust for power. He crossed the Rubicon river, marched on Rome, met Pompey at the Battle of Pharsalus, and won, even though his troops were outnumbered by Pompey's.

STABBED

After his victory, Caesar was made dictator of the empire for a period of 10 years. But then Caesar went one step further—he made himself dictator for life. He was extremely popular because of his conquering skills, but not *that* popular. Many people in Rome thought he'd taken too much power for himself. A group of Roman politicians decided to do something about it and stabbed him to death.

HARDOMETER

CUNNING: 8
COURAGE: 9
SURVIVAL SKILLS: 7
RUTHLESSNESS: 9

THE DUKE OF WELLINGTON

Wellington was one of Britain's best generals. He became famous for defeating the French revolutionary leader Napoleon at Waterloo.

BRITISH ARMY

Wellington was born in Dublin in 1769, to rich, Anglo-Irish parents. He joined the British army in 1787 and fought in India, where he won a series of victories and earned a reputation as a brilliant general who commanded his troops with firm discipline.

NAPOLEONIC WARS

In 1808, Wellington commanded the British, Portuguese, and Spanish armies in the Peninsula War. The war was part of a bigger conflict—the Napoleonic Wars. It was fought between France, which had recently had a revolution, and other countries in Europe that did not want revolutions themselves. They also wanted to put things back to the way they were in France before the revolution, with a king in charge. Coming from a wealthy and upper-class background, Wellington wholeheartedly agreed. He drove the French army out of Portugal and Spain, and became a British hero.

WATERLOO

In 1814, Napoleon was exiled to the island of Elba in the Mediterranean Sea. Wellington, meanwhile, was made a duke back in Britain. But in 1815, Napoleon escaped from his island and raised an army in France. Wellington immediately assembled the British army, and met Napoleon at the Battle of Waterloo in present-day Belgium. Wellington had the help of the Prussian army, and through a series of clever battle tactics, defeated the French for good. Napoleon was exiled again—somewhere much farther away this time—and Wellington became an even bigger hero in Britain.

PRIME MINISTER

While being a top British general, Wellington was also a politician. Once he'd won the Battle of Waterloo, he concentrated on politics. He became prime minister in 1828. But that didn't stop Wellington from fighting completely. In 1829, he had an argument with another politician, Lord Winchelsea. They decided that the only way to resolve the issue was by a duel with pistols in Battersea Park in London. They both missed—on purpose—but their honor was maintained.

HARDOMETER

CUNNING: 9
COURAGE: 8
SURVIVAL SKILLS: 8
RUTHLESSNESS: 8

MAHMUD OF GHAZNI

Mahmud was a hard as nails warrior who expanded the Ghaznavid Empire and relentlessly raided India.

HARD AS NAILS RATING: 8

GRABBING THE THRONE

Mahmud was born in 971 in what's now southeastern Afghanistan. His father died in 997, having conquered the empire of Ghazni. Mahmud was away when he heard about his father's death, and he was absolutely furious when he learned that his father had named his younger brother, Ismail, as heir. Mahmud wasn't going to let that happen. He marched east, captured the capital city of Ghazni, made himself king, and jailed his younger brother in his home for life.

GHAZNI GETS BIGGER

Mahmud wasn't happy with his empire as it was. He thought it needed to be bigger, so he led his cavalry and archers on a path of conquest, adding new lands in central and south Asia to the Ghaznavid Empire. By 1001, he'd conquered an impressive amount of lands. But it still wasn't enough for Mahmud.

HARDOMETER

CUNNING: 7
COURAGE: 8
SURVIVAL SKILLS: 8
RUTHLESSNESS: 9

RAIDING INDIA

Mahmud had his eye on India, and that same year he made the first of many raids into the Punjab, home of the fierce Rajputs. His quick cavalry outmaneuvered the elephant-mounted Rajput warriors, and Mahmud added chunks of northern India to his growing empire. Over the next 30 years, he made no fewer than 17 raids into northern India. Each time, Mahmud and his army returned home before the rainy season came and blocked their path back to Ghazni.

MAKING ENEMIES

As time went on, the relentless raiding and killing continued, but with extra looting because Mahmud's empire needed more funds. Mahmud ruthlessly targeted Hindu temples and stole their gold. In 1025, he captured Somnath and destroyed its beautiful temple. Fifty thousand people died defending Somnath, making Mahmud one of the most hated enemies of the Hindus ever.

GREAT GHAZNAVID EMPIRE

Mahmud loved to fight, but he also encouraged learning, and he made Ghazni into one of the cultural centers of the world. When he died in 1030, his empire stretched from what's now Afghanistan, through central Asia to Pakistan, and through northern India to the Indian Ocean on the coast of Gujarat. The empire was ruled by Mahmud's heirs for more than 150 years.

THE WORLD'S WORST WARS

All wars are terrible. They are full of violence, blood, and of course, death. One of the worst wars in history was the Second World War. Seventy million people died—the highest number of deaths of any war. Here are three other particularly bloody conflicts from throughout history.

THE NAPOLEONIC WARS

After the French Revolution, many European countries were at war with France. The French leader Napoleon led France to victory and defeat during this time. The most famous of these conflicts is the Battle of Waterloo (see page 25). The worst defeat of the Napoleonic Wars was the attack on Russia in 1812. Napoleon led an invasion force of 650,000 soldiers. They followed the Russian army, who burned everything behind them as they went, so that there was no food or shelter for the French. The bitterly cold Russian winter froze the exhausted, hungry French troops, who were attacked and defeated by the Russians. Only 40,000 French soldiers made it back to France.

THE RUSSIAN CIVIL WAR

After the Russian Revolution, which ended with the Bolsheviks in charge, Russia had a massive civil war from 1918 to 1921. As well as the Russian people involved on each side, other countries joined the opposition to the Bolsheviks because they didn't want revolutionaries in control. These soldiers formed the White Army. Bolshevik supporters formed the Red Army. If either side took prisoners, they were usually killed. The Red Army killed 50,000 White Army prisoners of war and civilians after they surrendered in one of the worst massacres of the civil war. After the war, Russia was in such a terrible mess that millions of people starved.

THE FIRST WORLD WAR

The First World War was fought between Britain, France, and their allies, including Canada and the United States, against Germany and its allies, from 1914 to 1918. Powerful new guns gouged enormous holes in the landscape, and soldiers were forced to take cover in trenches, which were often muddy, cramped, and full of rats. Battles had extremely high death tolls—on the first day of the Battle of the Somme in 1916, there were 60,000 dead and wounded British, Canadian, and other Commonwealth soldiers. Around 18 million people died in the First World War, and another 21 million were wounded.

JOAN OF ARC

HARD AS NAILS RATING: 7

Joan of Arc looked like a teenage farm girl instead of a warrior, but she led the entire French army to victory.

HUNDRED YEARS WAR

When Joan was born, around 1412, a long, bitter war was raging on for control of France. On one side were the Burgundians, who were English allies, and on the other side were supporters of Charles the Dauphin, who claimed the French throne. One half of Joan's village was controlled by the Burgundians, and the other half by Charles's supporters.

VOICES FROM GOD

Joan started hearing voices when she was about 13. She believed they belonged to Christian saints, who began to make some very difficult demands. They told her to help Charles the Dauphin and get rid of the Burgundians. This was difficult for a farmer's daughter to pull off, but Joan felt she had to do what the voices told her.

JOAN THE KNIGHT

HARDOMETER

CUNNING: 7
COURAGE: 9
SURVIVAL SKILLS: 5
RUTHLESSNESS: 7

Incredible though it might seem, Joan managed to get a meeting with Charles, and then to persuade him that he needed her help. She was dressed as a knight, put on a horse, and sent off to fight at the city of Orleans, which was besieged by the English and their allies. Even though she'd never fought in a war before, Joan became a heroine almost overnight. She fought bravely and cleverly, and the English were defeated. For her part in the victory, Joan was put in charge of the entire French army, alongside the Duke of Alençon.

KING CHARLES

Joan seemed to have a knack for leading an army. She led the French against the Burgundians, chasing them out of one town after another and defeating them in battle. The French did so well that Charles was crowned king of France.

CAPTURE

In 1430, Joan was captured by the Burgundians. She escaped twice, but finally stood trial at a church court in 1431. The court found Joan guilty of being a witch, and she was burned at the stake. She's now a saint in the Roman Catholic Church.

HONGWU

Hongwu fought his way from being a starving peasant to a powerful warlord, and finally emperor of the whole of China.

HARD AS NAILS RATING: 9

A HARD LIFE

When Hongwu was born in 1328, the Yuan dynasty ruled China. The dynasty had begun with Genghis Khan's grandson, Kublai Khan. For peasants like Hongwu, life was hard—there was widespread drought and famine, and millions of people died of starvation. Rebel peasants formed bands of warriors and robbed rich families. They shared what they'd stolen among the poor, like Chinese Robin Hoods.

THE RED TURBANS

Hongwu joined a rebel band known as the Red Turbans, led by Guo Zixing. Hongwu was tough and clever, and he quickly rose to be second-in-command of Guo's rebel army. He captured cities and expanded the rebel army, and when Guo died in 1355, Hongwu took over as leader.

CHINESE LEADER

HARDOMETER

CUNNING: 9
COURAGE: 9
SURVIVAL SKILLS: 9
RUTHLESSNESS: 9

After a lot more fighting, Hongwu's empire grew. He captured the important and wealthy city of Nanjing, and used it as his base. Rather than just being a rebel leader, he said he was the leader of the whole Chinese nation against the Yuan, and other rebel leaders either submitted to him or were killed.

But there were some rebel leaders who wanted to rule China, too. One of them was Chen Youliang, who ruled a large chunk of central China. In 1363, Hongwu fought him in a three-day battle on Lake Poyang. Hongwu won, Chen died, and his large fleet was destroyed. Hongwu took over Chen's territory and captured other provinces.

MIGHTY MING

Now Hongwu had control of most of the south of China. He sent two of his generals to lead his army against the north. In 1368 he proclaimed himself emperor of a new dynasty, called the Ming. He took the name Hongwu, meaning vastly martial— before that he'd been plain old Zhu Yuanzhang. Eleven years later, he finally controlled the whole of China, plus Korea. Hongwu ruled as emperor for 30 years, but he was suspicious of people plotting against him, and had thousands killed. He died in 1398, but the Ming dynasty lasted until 1644.

ALEXANDER THE GREAT

Alexander the Great was the king of Macedonia, and he very quickly became the ruler of a vast empire. He led a conquering army that was never defeated.

KING OF MACEDONIA

The kingdom of Macedonia rose to be the most powerful nation in the ancient Greek world. The empire included most of Greece. Alexander became its king in 336 BCE, when he was 20 years old. His father had been murdered, and Alexander lost no time in killing his father's assassins, along with anyone he felt was a rival to his leadership. When the Greek city-state of Thebes dared to revolt against Macedonian rule, Alexander destroyed the city, killed thousands, and sold everyone else into slavery. Now everyone knew it was a mistake to mess with Alexander.

PLACES TO CONQUER

POUNDING THE PERSIANS

Alexander planned to expand his territory, and he had his eye on the huge Persian Empire—the largest empire in the world at the time. He attacked the Persian army in Asia Minor (modern-day Turkey), then Persian lands in the Mediterranean and Egypt. Over the course of several battles, he defeated the Persian leader, Darius III, even though in one battle Alexander's army was half the size of the Persian army. King Darius ran away, and Alexander was proclaimed the king of Asia. Then he conquered Susa, the capital of Persia, and Babylon, securing control of the whole Persian Empire.

ALEXANDER'S UNBEATABLE ARMY

Alexander now had a taste for conquering, and he was very good at it. He continued eastward, capturing new land as he went. He traveled thousands of miles into central Asia, and continued farther into what's now Pakistan and India, where he defeated King Porus and his war elephants. The battles fought by Alexander's army always ended in victory. By the time he'd finished fighting, Alexander had founded more than 70 cities.

SUDDEN ENDING

Finally, Alexander headed home, celebrating his victories, massive amounts of treasure, and an empire that now stretched from the Mediterranean to the Himalayas. After an especially big celebration in Babylon, Alexander died suddenly, when he was just 32. In the 12 years of his rule, he'd conquered an empire that covered most of the known world—more than one million square miles (three million km^2). After his death, Alexander's generals took over different parts of the empire.

HARDOMETER

CUNNING: 8
COURAGE: 8
SURVIVAL SKILLS: 8
RUTHLESSNESS: 9

WAR GAME

For two to six players, you'll need a game piece for each player and one die to play this game.

BEGIN YOUR PATH OF DESTRUCTION HERE.

2

Attack and capture an enemy fortress. Go forward three spaces.

12

Ambushed by your enemies. Go back two spaces.

10

13

Defeated in battle. Go back two spaces.

15

16

24

23

Besieged by enemy troops. Miss a turn.

Mortally wounded in battle. Go back to the start.

Capture new territory, and loot tons of treasure. Roll again.

27

You're fierce and fearless warriors in the mood for a battle. You want to conquer as much land and terrify as many people as possible. But which of you will be tough enough to conquer a massive empire?

4

Disease ravages your troops. Go back three spaces.

6

Brilliant military tactics defeat the enemy. Go forward two spaces.

EXILE

Forced into exile by power-hungry relatives. Miss a turn.

9

Win a historic victory. Roll again.

18

Miss a turn while you crush a rebellion.

21

Capture the enemy's capital city. Go forward four spaces.

Another awesome victory over your foes. Go forward two spaces.

29

Congratulations! You have conquered a vast empire. Now you just have to avoid assassination.

BOUDICA

After the ancient Romans invaded Britain, some brave Britons rebelled against them. One of them was the fierce warrior queen, Boudica.

HARD AS NAILS RATING: 7.5

ROTTEN ROMANS

Boudica was queen of the Iceni, in what's now eastern England. The Romans had allowed her husband, King Prasutagus, to rule the Iceni after they were conquered. But when Prasutagus died, in around 60 CE, they decided to take control themselves. They attacked Boudica and her daughters, and threw the Iceni people off their land. But they hadn't counted on Queen Boudica—she wasn't the kind of woman to let them get away with it.

REBEL VICTORY

Boudica led the Iceni in a rebellion against the Romans. They were joined by other British warriors who were equally angry with the invaders. The rebel army, complete with horse-drawn war chariots, headed for the Roman fort at Colchester, which was the Roman capital of Britain at the time. Hungry for revenge, Boudica and her rebel army defeated the Roman ninth legion and destroyed the fort.

HARDOMETER

CUNNING: 7
COURAGE: 9
SURVIVAL SKILLS: 7
RUTHLESSNESS: 7

LONDON'S BURNING

Next, Boudica and her brave band of rebels headed for London, which was then a small trading settlement. She was hoping for a fight with the forces of Suetonius, the Roman governor of Britain, but they retreated. So instead Boudica smashed and burned London, and then marched north and did the same thing in Saint Albans.

FINAL BATTLE

Boudica did not have much opposition at first. But Suetonius was preparing his Roman forces, and he marched them to meet Boudica. The two armies met somewhere in the middle of England—no one is sure exactly where. Boudica's army put up a strong fight, but they were defeated by the Romans, who attacked with a hail of spears, then drove the British army back and trapped them. Boudica's army was finally crushed. According to legend, Boudica wasn't killed in the battle, but she poisoned herself to avoid being captured and shamed by her Roman enemies.

NAPOLEON

Napoleon Bonaparte led revolutionary France to war against the powerful countries of Europe, and succeeded— for a while.

HARD AS NAILS RATING: 8

REVOLUTION AND REBELLION

The French Revolution began in 1789, as the result of an unfair system in France that meant wealthy people lived in luxury while the poor starved. Napoleon was a 20-year-old French army officer at the time. He supported the revolution, and led his troops against French rebels who joined forces with foreign troops in Toulon. Napoleon defeated them, and became a revolutionary hero.

NAPOLEON VS THE WORLD

Many European countries wanted to stop the French Revolution, because they were worried it could spread. The people in charge liked things just the way they were. Hard as nails Napoleon was just the man to stand up to them. He was given command of the French army and fought the Austrians and their allies. He defeated them and forced them to make peace. But at the Battle of the Nile, British admiral Lord Nelson defeated him.

CUNNING: 8
COURAGE: 8
SURVIVAL SKILLS: 8
RUTHLESSNESS: 8

INVASION PLANS

Napoleon wasn't happy with the way things were run in France, so he took control in 1804 and made himself emperor. He decided that invasion was the best way forward, but he was stopped from invading Britain at the Battle of Trafalgar—by Lord Nelson again. Napoleon was more successful with conquering other parts of Europe. He installed friends and relatives to run them, making France the most powerful nation in Europe. But then his army suffered a massive defeat when it tried to invade Russia. Hundreds of thousands of French soldiers were killed by the Russians, or starved or froze to death.

SURRENDER AND EXILE

Napoleon had to surrender. He was banished to the island of Elba in the Mediterranean. The old ways began to return to France, and Napoleon simply had to do something about it. In 1815, he escaped from Elba, marched on Paris, and gathered an army. Things were going well until the Battle of Waterloo, where Napoleon was defeated for the last time, by the British Duke of Wellington (see page 24). He was captured and exiled again—this time to a really remote island, Saint Helena in the South Atlantic. He died there in 1821.

TOMYRIS

Tomyris was a warrior queen who refused to be intimidated by the biggest empire in the world.

HAVING FRIENDS FOR DINNER

Tomyris was the queen of the Massagetae, hard as nails people who lived in central Asia. According to an ancient historian, they had some unusual customs. Apparently, when men got old they were killed and eaten. It was considered a privilege to be eaten!

CYRUS THE CONQUEROR

In 530 BCE, Cyrus the Great, ruler of the huge Persian Empire, realized he'd forgotten to conquer the Massagetae, and decided to do something about it. His first attempt at grabbing the Massagetae lands was to propose marriage to Tomyris. She turned him down, so Cyrus prepared for invasion. He began building a bridge across to the Massagetae territory. Tomyris wasn't worried and she sent Cyrus a message, saying if he wanted a fight he could pick which side of the river to have it on.

TRICKY PERSIANS

The Persians played a sneaky trick: they left their main camp with a small number of soldiers to guard it, while the rest of the army moved elsewhere. Massagetae soldiers, led by Tomyris's son, Spargapises, found the camp, killed all the soldiers, and started on the food and wine that the Persians had left for them. Then they all had a little snooze. That was when the Persian army arrived and killed everyone except Spargapises, who they took as their prisoner.

TOMYRIS GETS ANGRY

Tomyris demanded that Cyrus release her son, promising a big fight if he didn't. Cyrus ignored her, and Spargapises killed himself in shame. When Tomyris found out, she was very sad and completely furious. She led her army against the Persians—the mightiest conquering army in the world at the time—and won.

A GRUESOME ENDING

Cyrus was killed in the battle. The story goes that Tomyris dipped his severed head in an animal skin full of blood, saying that he could have his fill of bloodshed. Then she kept his skull as a drinking cup. We don't know what happened to Tomyris herself— maybe she had many happy years drinking from her enemy's skull!

HARDOMETER

CUNNING: 9
COURAGE: 9
SURVIVAL SKILLS: 10
RUTHLESSNESS: 9

SHI HUANGDI

Shi Huangdi had to do a lot of fighting, but eventually he united the different Chinese states into one country, and became its first emperor.

HARD AS NAILS RATING: 7.8

POWER STRUGGLES

When Shi Huangdi became king of the state of Qin (pronounced "chin") in 246 BCE, there were seven states within China that were constantly at war. Shi Huangdi decided that everyone would be much better off if all the states became one united China, with him in charge of them all. Unfortunately, the leaders of the other states had similar ideas. By 221 BCE, after nine years of fighting, Shi Huangdi had achieved his ambition. He gave himself the name Qin Shi Huangdi, which means first majestic and divine emperor of Qin. The name China comes from Shi Huangdi's home state.

KEEPING IT TOGETHER

Shi Huangdi wanted to make sure his united China stayed that way, so he made everyone use the same language, money, weights, and measurements. He changed the way the country was divided, too, so that the old regions didn't exist anymore. And he decided his unified country should do some conquering—he added a large chunk of land to the south of China, the area that's now Vietnam.

HARDOMETER

CUNNING: 7
COURAGE: 7
SURVIVAL SKILLS: 8
RUTHLESSNESS: 9

GREAT WALL

In the north, though, Shi Huangdi didn't manage to conquer anything. In fact, northern invaders looked as though they might do some conquering of their own, so Shi Huangdi had a massive wall built to keep them out. The wall doesn't exist today—another Great Wall of China was built much later, in the Ming dynasty—but hundreds of thousands of workers died from hunger and exhaustion building Shi Huangdi's wall.

ETERNAL WARRIORS

China's first emperor began acting oddly as time went on. He searched for the elixir of eternal life, but he didn't find it; he ordered all books to be burned, with a few exceptions, such as the books in his own library; and he had hundreds of scholars buried alive. When he died in 210 BCE, Shi Huangdi was buried in an extremely impressive grave. It was a vast underground tomb filled with life-sized warriors and horses made from terra-cotta. While Qin didn't succeed in his search for eternal life, his terra-cotta army lived for thousands of years.

CHOOSE YOUR WEAPON

You can't be a warrior without a weapon. It could be something as simple as a rock (for Stone Age warriors), or as sophisticated as a cannon. Below are a few hard as nails weapons that have been used throughout history.

TREBUCHET

If you're a medieval warrior with a city to besiege, you need one of these. They're similar to giant catapults, with a long arm that has a container at one end and a heavy weight at the other. Simply place the missile of your choice—such as rocks, severed heads, or horse manure—in the container, let the weight pull down the arm, and fling the missile at your target. Perfect for battering city walls.

BOW AND ARROW

The bow and arrow was one of the first weapons to be invented. It requires a lot of skill. They're an ideal choice if you're a member of a Mongolian horde, although you will need to be an expert horse rider as well as an accurate archer. Longbows are the most effective, and they can even beat crossbows if you're skillful enough.

WAR CHARIOT

These two-wheeled carts have been around for thousands of years. This chariot is a must-have for a skilled ancient Egyptian horseman or perhaps a Celt who wants to defeat the Romans. A team with an archer and deadly blades fixed to the wheel axles of the chariot really show the enemy who's boss.

SAMURAI SWORD

If you really want to terrify your enemies, wielding a samurai sword should do the trick, especially if you're dressed in full samurai clothing. These long, curved, elaborately decorated swords are held with two hands.

GREEK FIRE

If you're a seventeenth-century Byzantine warrior and you want the element of surprise, you need Greek fire. Today, no one's sure what it actually was—maybe a mixture of sulfur, charcoal, quicklime, and fuel—but it terrified the enemies of the Byzantine Empire because it was impossible to put out and even burned on water. It was thrown in pots (like hand grenades) or shot through tubes.

CANNON

These powerful weapons replaced trebuchets for bombarding castles and cities. You will also find them useful in sea battles, too. However, loading and firing heavy cannons can be a dangerous business.

CHARLEMAGNE

HARD AS NAILS RATING: 8

Charlemagne was a medieval warrior king who conquered most of western Europe for the first time since the ancient Romans.

FRANKISH KINGDOM

Charlemagne became the king of the Franks in 768. At first, he ruled with his brother, but he was on his own from 771, after his brother died. The Franks had battled the Romans hundreds of years before, then settled in modern-day France. Over the years, the Frankish kingdom grew as it conquered more and more territory, until in Charlemagne's time it covered most of what's now France, plus Belgium, Austria, and a few other parts of Europe.

SAXON WARS

Charlemagne strongly believed that the kingdom of Saxony (now northwest Germany) should be part of his own kingdom. The Saxons disagreed, also very strongly. Charlemagne's war with the Saxons continued for more than 30 long years. There were 18 major battles and many thousands of deaths. In 782, Charlemagne killed 4,500 Saxon prisoners of war on the same day. In the end, in 804, Charlemagne won. The Saxons had been quite happy with their own religion, but Charlemagne made them choose between becoming Christians or being killed.

HARDOMETER

CUNNING: 8
COURAGE: 8
SURVIVAL SKILLS: 8
RUTHLESSNESS: 8

THE FRANKS SPREAD OUT

The war with Saxony didn't stop Charlemagne from getting involved in other fights at the same time. His father had helped the pope fight the troublesome Lombards, and when a different pope asked Charlemagne for help against the same enemy, he felt he couldn't say no. It also provided a great conquering opportunity: Charlemagne battered the Lombards and added Lombardy (now part of northern Italy) to his kingdom. Somehow, Charlemagne also found the time to conquer chunks of what's now Germany and Austria, as well as some of the land bordering his kingdom in the Pyrenees. He gained vast new territories and enormous wealth.

HOLY ROMANS

Charlemagne helped Pope Leo III defeat a rebellion against him. In return, Leo gave Charlemagne land in the middle of Italy, and Charlemagne became emperor of the Romans in 800. When he died in 814, Charlemagne had united most of western Europe in the Holy Roman Empire.

TOMOE GOZEN

Tomoe Gozen was a female Japanese samurai warrior, who fought bravely and became a legendary heroine.

HARD AS NAILS
RATING: 7.5

SCARY SAMURAI

Samurai were originally bodyguards for Japanese lords. They became a class of warriors, famous for their ferocity and the code they lived by, called "bushido." It was based on self-discipline, loyalty, and honor. They looked terrifying with their elaborate armor and huge swords. Among the many male samurai, there were a small number of women. Tomoe Gozen was one of the fiercest and most famous, although it's impossible to tell which parts of her story are true and which are invented.

RIVAL CLANS

Tomoe Gozen took part in the Gempei War, fought from 1180 to 1185 between two rival clans, the Taira and the Minamoto. Tomoe Gozen went into battle alongside Minamoto Yoshinaka, her lord and possibly her husband, against the Taira. She was quite a warrior: skilled in horse riding, martial arts, archery, and swordsmanship, she was also very beautiful and as hard as nails.

ENEMY HEAD

In one battle, so the story goes, Tomoe Gozen defended a bridge single-handedly. In another, she cut off the head of a Taira leader who tried to drag her from her horse, then presented his head to Minamoto Yoshinaka. Yoshinaka was killed near the end of the Gempei War at the Battle of Awazu, but Tomoe Gozen is supposed to have survived it, although the Minamoto clan lost the battle.

A MYSTERIOUS ENDING

There are different stories about what happened to Tomoe Gozen in the end. One story says she became a concubine, or a sort of second-class wife, of the enemy leader, and later became a nun. Another story says that after the Battle of Awazu, rather than face capture, she committed "seppuku," which is a gruesome method of suicide by plunging the samurai sword into the stomach. In another gruesome alternative ending, Tomoe Gozen found Yoshinaka's head on the battlefield and carried it with her as she walked into the sea and drowned herself.

HARDOMETER

CUNNING: 7
COURAGE: 9
SURVIVAL SKILLS: 6
RUTHLESSNESS: 8

TIMUR

Timur was one of the most ruthless conquerors in history. His career as a hard as nails warrior lasted nearly 40 years.

TAKING TRANSOXANIA

Timur lived near Samarkand in Transoxania (modern-day Uzbekistan), which was ruled by a neighboring leader. Timur was made minister of Transoxania under its ruler, Ilyas Khoja, but instead he joined forces with his brother-in-law. They attacked Khoja and captured Transoxania. Then he had his brother-in-law assassinated. Timur was finally in charge.

CONQUESTS

Timur fought and conquered neighboring states, and supported the leader of the Crimea against the Russians and other enemies by occupying Moscow and defeating the Lithuanians. But his conquering career really got going in the Middle East and central Asia: over a period of about 10 years, he captured large parts of what's now Iran, Iraq, Armenia, Azerbaijan, Georgia, and Turkey, leaving destruction in his wake. Timur wasn't the sort of conqueror who appreciated beautiful cities and ancient sites—if it was in his way, he smashed it.

HARDOMETER

CUNNING: 9
COURAGE: 9
SURVIVAL SKILLS: 9
RUTHLESSNESS: 10

THE GOLDEN HORDE

You wouldn't have thought he'd have time, but while all that conquering was going on, Timur was also fighting Tokhtamysh, leader of the Golden Horde, from the western part of the old Mongol Empire. Tokhtamysh was constantly invading land Timur had conquered, which made Timur very angry. After a series of victories and defeats, Timur finally beat Tokhtamysh in 1395. While Timur was away defeating Tokhtamysh, revolts in Persia were ruthlessly crushed by Timur's troops, who destroyed cities, massacred people, and built gruesome towers from their skulls.

DEATH AND DESTRUCTION

Nowhere was safe. In 1398, Timur attacked India, reduced the city of Delhi to ruins, and used elephants to carry away tons of loot. His path of destruction included the cities of Aleppo and Damascus in Syria, and Baghdad in modern-day Iraq, where he massacred 20,000 people. Timur was turning his attention to China when he was finally stopped, not by an invading army, but by a fatal illness. The vast lands Timur had conquered were split among his sons and grandsons, who argued about the divided empire until it was finally reunited by Timur's youngest son.

ATTILA THE HUN

Attila led a terrifying army of Huns, the toughest of the warriors who fought the Roman army at the end of the Roman Empire in the west.

BARBARIAN HORDES

The Huns were barbarians, which at the time of the Roman Empire didn't necessarily mean uncivilized thugs—it just meant anyone who wasn't Roman. The Huns came from central Asia and, like the Mongols, they were skilled horsemen who were terrifying in battle, shooting arrows and throwing javelins from horseback with deadly accuracy.

HUGE HUNNIC EMPIRE

In 434, Attila became joint king of the Huns with his brother, Bleda. They ruled together until Attila decided there was only room for one king and had his brother murdered in 445. By the time Attila ruled the Huns, there was a massive Hunnic Empire, covering great swaths of eastern Europe and central Asia. But Attila wasn't the sort of leader to leave it at that. The Roman Empire was divided into eastern and western parts. Attila attacked the Eastern Roman Empire, which had its capital in Constantinople (modern-day Istanbul in Turkey), and demanded huge amounts of gold.

HARDOMETER

CUNNING: 9
COURAGE: 8
SURVIVAL SKILLS: 9
RUTHLESSNESS: 10

ATTACKS ON GAUL AND ITALY

Having caused as much trouble as possible in the Eastern Roman Empire, Atilla turned to the Western Roman Empire. In 451 and 452, he attacked Gaul (modern-day France and Belgium), but he wasn't as successful as he'd hoped. He was forced to retreat from Gaul when the Romans joined forces with the Visigoths and defeated the Huns. His attacks in Italy ended in disaster when his army was ravaged by disease. Still, he'd managed to do a lot of rampaging, destroying, and looting in the meantime.

END OF AN EMPIRE

In 453, Attila's rampaging days came to an end. The story goes that he died after having a nosebleed on one of his many wedding nights (Attila married many women). It might have been an illness that killed him, but it's also possible that he was murdered. After Attila died, his sons fought over who should succeed him, and the Hunnic Empire broke up.

WARRIOR QUIZ

Take this quiz and find out how much you know about the warriors in this book.

1. Which warrior united the Mongolians and conquered an empire?

a) Attila the Hun

b) Charlemagne

c) Genghis Khan

2. Which queen defeated Cyrus the Great?

a) Boudica

b) Artemisia

c) Tomyris

3. Which Roman governor of Britain did Boudica fight?

a) Julius Caesar

b) Suetonius

c) Cicero

4. How long did the Trung sisters rule Vietnam?

a) 30 years

b) Three years

c) Three months

5. Which country did King Piye of Kush conquer?

a) Egypt

b) Persia

c) Syria

6. Who was defeated by Julius Caesar at the Battle of Pharsalus?

a) Mark Antony

b) Crassus

c) Pompey

7. Who was exiled to the island of Saint Helena?

a) Napoleon

b) Alexander the Great

c) Charlemagne

8. Which empire was conquered by Babur?

a) Ottoman Empire

b) Moghul Empire

c) Persian Empire

9. Which of these warriors died in battle?

a) Alexander the Great

b) Attila the Hun

c) Cyrus the Great

10. Who became the first emperor of the Ming dynasty?

a) Shihuangdi

b) Hongwu

c) Taizong

Answers: 1 c, 2 c, 3 b, 4 b, 5 a, 6 c, 7 a, 8 b, 9 c, 10 b

HARD AS NAILS WARRIORS TIMELINE

761 BCE

King Piye of Kush conquered Egypt.

559 BCE

Cyrus the Great became the king of Persia, and went on to create a huge Persian Empire.

530 BCE

Tomyris, queen of the Massagetae, defeated and killed Cyrus the Great.

336 BCE

Alexander the Great became the king of Macedonia and quickly conquered a vast empire.

246 BCE

Shi Huangdi became the king of Qin. Before long, he united China and became its first emperor.

100 BCE

Julius Caesar, who almost became the first emperor of ancient Rome, was born.

40 CE

The Trung sisters drove the Chinese invaders out of Vietnam, and ruled the country themselves—for a while, at least.

PLACES TO CONQUER

61 CE

Boudica, the queen of the Iceni people in Britain, died after her army was defeated by the ancient Romans.

434 CE

Attila became the king of the Huns, the most feared of the barbarians in the dying days of the Roman Empire in the west.

768 CE

Charlemagne became the king of the Franks, and expanded his empire until it stretched into Italy.

997 CE

Mahmud of Ghazni became king of the Ghaznavid Empire in central Asia.

1185 CE

Female samurai warrior Tomoe Gozen fought in the Gempei War in Japan.

1206 CE

Genghis Khan united the Mongols and became their universal leader. Then he conquered the second-biggest empire in the history of the world.

1328 CE

Hongwu was born in China. He was a starving peasant, but went on to become the first Ming emperor of China.

1336 CE

Ruthless conqueror Timur was born. His empire eventually stretched from India and Russia to the Mediterranean Sea.

1412 CE

Joan of Arc, the teenage farm girl who led the French army, was born around this date.

1495 CE

Babur became ruler of Farghana in central Asia. He went on to found the Moghul Empire in India.

1769 CE

British general the Duke of Wellington was born. His most famous victory was at Waterloo, where he defeated Napoleon, but he was also the British prime minister.

1804 CE

French revolutionary leader Napoleon became emperor of France.

1829 CE

Apache warrior Geronimo was born.

LEARNING MORE

BOOKS

Bergin, Mark. *Warfare in the Ancient World*. Peter Bedrick Books, 2003.

Steele, Tara. *Medieval Warfare*. Crabtree Publishing, 2004.

Woods, Michael. *Ancient Warfare Technology: From Javelins to Chariots*. Twenty-First Century Books, 2011.

EDUCATIONAL WEBSITES

Ancient History
(History Channel):
**www.history.com/
topics/ancient-history**

Ancient History
Encyclopedia:
www.ancient.eu

History (BBC):
**www.bbc.co.uk/history/
ancient**

GLOSSARY

ASSASSIN Someone who kills people for political reasons

BARBARIANS People who were considered uncivilized and primitive by the ancient Romans

BUSHIDO The way of samurai life

CAVALRY Soldiers on horseback

CIVIL WAR War between groups of people from the same country or state

CONCUBINE A woman who is in a relationship with a man, but is not his wife

DICTATOR A leader who takes total power and authority

DROMEDARY A type of camel that has one hump

DUEL A fight between two people, usually to the death

DYNASTY A series of rulers from the same family

ELIXIR A clear, sweet liquid taken as a medicine

EMPIRE A group of states or countries ruled by one leader or state

EXILE Banned from your native country

MASSACRED Brutally killed

PHARAOHS Leaders of ancient Egypt

PROVINCES Regions of land that belong to a country or empire

RAMPAGING Behaving in a violent or angry way

REBELLION A breakaway from or resistance to authority

RESERVATION A limited area of land where Native nations live

REVOLTING Rebelling

REVOLUTION An overthrow of a leader

SAMURAI Military noblemen of Japan

SETTLERS People who move to a new area and set up home there permanently

SIEGE Surround a city or town with the aim of capturing it

SURRENDER To give yourself up (or give up control of something)

TACTIC A plan or system

TERRA-COTTA A type of earthenware made of clay; the word means "baked earth"

TREBUCHET A huge type of catapult

INDEX